D1252799

101.4
B611o

DISCARD

Phillips Library
Bethany College

DISCARD

ON PHILOSOPHICAL STYLE

ON
PHILOSOPHICAL STYLE

by

BRAND BLANSHARD

GREENWOOD PRESS, PUBLISHERS
NEW YORK

Originally published in 1954
by the Indiana University Press.

First Greenwood Reprinting 1969

Library of Congress Catalogue Card Number 69-13830

SBN 8371-1975-8

PRINTED IN UNITED STATES OF AMERICA

LORD MACAULAY once recorded in his diary a memorable attempt—his first and apparently also his last—to read Kant's *Critique* : " I received today a translation of Kant. . . . I tried to read it, but found it utterly unintelligible, just as if it had been written in Sanscrit. Not one word of it gave me anything like an idea except a Latin quotation from Persius. It seems to me that it ought to be possible to explain a true theory of metaphysics in words that I can understand. I can understand Locke, and Berkeley, and Hume, and Reid, and Stewart. I can understand Cicero's Academics, and most of Plato ; and it seems odd that in a book on the elements of metaphysics . . . I should not be able to comprehend a word."

What sort of writing was it that Macaulay was called upon to read ? I quote a single fairly typical sentence : " Because a certain form of sensuous intuition exists in the mind *à priori* which rests on the receptivity of the

1

101.4
B611b

representative faculty (sensibility), the understanding, as a spontaneity, is able to determine the internal sense by means of the diversity of given representations, conformably to the synthetical unity of apperception, and thus to cogitate the synthetical unity of the apperception of the manifold of sensuous intuition *à priori*, as the condition to which must necessarily be submitted all objects of human intuition."

In a recent book Hans Reichenbach records a similar adventure with his illustrious fellow-countryman, Hegel. He picked up Hegel's *Philosophy of History* and, before getting past the introduction, read the following : " Reason is substance, as well as infinite power, its own infinite material underlying all the natural and spiritual life ; as also the infinite form which sets the material in motion. Reason is the substance from which all things derive their being." Now, says Reichenbach, " the term ' reason,' as generally used, means an abstract capacity of human beings, manifesting itself in their behaviour, or to be modest, in

2

parts of their behaviour. Does the philosopher quoted wish to say that our bodies are
made of an abstract capacity of themselves ?
Even a philosopher cannot mean such an
absurdity. What then does he mean ? "
Reichenbach discusses it for two pages, but
gives it up as hopeless.

I venture to give another example. One of
the most eminent philosophers of this century
conceived logic as the theory of inquiry, and
it was therefore important for him to define
inquiry in the clearest possible terms. He
thought much about it, and finally offered this
as the considered result : " Inquiry is the con-
trolled or directed transformation of an inde-
terminate situation into one that is so deter-
minate in its constituent distinctions and
relations as to convert the elements of the
original situation into a unified whole."
Bertrand Russell, having to comment on this
definition, points out that, far from distinguishing clearly one intellectual process from
others, it could be taken with at least equal
propriety as describing a sergeant drilling

a group of recruits, or a bricklayer laying bricks.

Here are three philosophers of the highest standing writing on subjects of which they were masters. And here are three readers of the highest intelligence who have to confess that to them the philosophers seem to be talking gibberish. How is this failure in communication to be explained?

There are various ways of explaining it. One way, not unpopular to-day, is to say that philosophy *is* gibberish, and that if readers generally had the courage and intelligence of these three, they too would call a spade a spade. This theory has its points, and under other circumstances I should like to pause over it. Unfortunately the people who hold it commonly go on to defend it by philosophizing about it, and very lucidly too, which shows, unless I am mistaken, that one *can* philosophize without gibberish, and that their theory needs amendment. Then there is the explanation that philosophy, like mathematics and theoretical physics, is a very difficult business,

4

that nothing can render abstract and sustained thought easy, and that it is really absurd to demand of the philosopher that he should be intelligible to men whose intelligence—to use a phrase of Principal Caird's—must be supplemented by a surgical operation. All this seems to be true. Philosophy *is* hard, in ways that we must consider in a moment. But again the defence overlooks too much, this time including history. Hard as philosophy is, there have been writers who have actually succeeded in making it intelligible and even exciting, not to the exceptionally gifted alone, but to a wide public. Socrates talked it, and Plato wrote it, in a way that some millions of readers have not been willing to forget. Bergson, without once descending to vulgarity, made it for a time one of the excitements of Paris. The British tradition in philosophy has been exceptionally fertile in writers with the gift of making crooked things straight. So if a philosophical writer cannot be followed, the difficulty of his subject can be pleaded only in mitigation of his offence,

5

not in condonation of it. There are too many expert witnesses on the other side.

Nevertheless, in this matter of style philosophy is in a difficult position. The trouble is that it belongs to the literature of knowledge, but that people demand of it all the virtues of the literature of power. Philosophizing proper is a purely intellectual enterprise. Its business is to analyse fundamental concepts, such as self, matter, mind, good, truth; to examine fundamental assumptions, such as that all events have causes; and to fit the conclusions together into a coherent view of nature and man's place in it. Now this is an austerely intellectual business. To be sure, philosophy must take account of values, and in the appropriate fields it has much to say of beauty and deformity, of good and evil, and of the issues of religious belief. But it is pledged to discuss these issues with scientific detachment and dispassionateness.

Yet in trying to do so the philosopher feels a tension that the scientist seldom has occasion to feel. There are three reasons for this. In the first place, his problems—at least the greatest of them—engage very deeply men's hopes and fears. No one opens a book on algebra with anxiety as to whether the author is going to treat the binomial theorem roughly, or a book of physics with the feeling that hope will be blighted if Ohm's law comes out badly. But people do feel that it is of importance whether their religious belief is honeycombed, or their hope of survival blasted, or even whether pleasure is made out to be the only good.

Secondly, because they feel these issues to be so important practically and emotionally, they are not contented unless the philosopher shows some sense of this too. No one would expect that as the proof of the binomial theorem comes in sight, the mathematician should go off into a little purple patch of triumph and relief, or that the physicist should give us Ohm's law in a burst of exultation. These things were exciting to their discoverers; perhaps they are to their expositors; but for all that most of us care, both formulae could be abandoned to-morrow, and to write about them as if men's hopes and fears were visibly hanging on them would be absurd. But on the great issues of philosophy many of men's hopes and fears do hang, and plain men feel that their philosopher should be alive to this and show it. It is not that they want him to give up his intellectual rigour and scrupulousness—at least they do not think that it is ; it is rather that when men with hearts as well as heads are dealing with themes of human importance, they should not deal with them as if nothing but their heads, and somewhat desiccated heads at that, were involved.

Thirdly, because these problems are humanly so important, plain men make a further demand on the philosopher. They want him to speak about them in such a way that they can overhear and, so far as practicable, understand. Academic tradition makes no requirement of this kind ; indeed, in some quarters there seems to be a presumption that anyone who writes in such a way as to be understood of the many is debasing the coinage of scholarship. But plain men do not see why this should be true, and, being one of them, neither do I. Indeed I think it an inversion of the truth. *Noblesse oblige*, in scholarship as elsewhere. In other fields, when a man amasses much that others do not have but want and need, this is supposed to place some obligation on him to consider those wants and needs. Why should this not hold also in the realm of the mind ? No doubt if there is such an obligation, it holds with different force in different regions. I do not know why a biologist, presenting a paper on a technical point to colleagues, should not write in a way as unintelligible as he pleases to those outside the circle, provided it is no obstacle to those inside. But suppose that his subject is one of general interest, that the session is open to the public and that he knows many of his audience will be drawn from that public. Should he then travel the same high and unheeding road ? No murmur may come from these visitors if he does. They have been told that he is a man of very great knowledge, presenting a subject that is deep, dark, and difficult; and when he reaches his impressively ncomprehensible close, they may tiptoe respectfully out, reflecting a little sadly that in spite of their interest and effort, these matters are quite beyond them. And so, of course, they may be. So far as they are, the situation will not concern us here. But they are not always so. Sometimes, to anyone who really knows what is going on, it is obvious that in the arts of presentation the learned speaker is almost illiterate, sometimes that, though not illiterate, he thinks that only substance matters and form can take care of itself, sometimes again that he is merely exhibiting bad manners in a region where he does not suspect there are any manners. He would not whisper a fascinating titbit of information to one friend while another who is equally interested is present, but he feels no hesitation in talking to an audience in a language lost on half of them. The French, who have earned a right to speak on these matters, have a saying in point : *La clarté est la politesse.* In philosophical speaking and writing, one's manners are connected very intimately with one's manner.

Unhappily, an awareness of this only increases the tension within the philosopher between thinker and writer. This tension grows from the double fact that feeling is the life of style, and yet that in philosophy it is generally an impertinence and a danger. Suppose that, as a person concerned to lift one's prose a notch above M. Jourdain's, one asks oneself who are the writers that have managed to make their ideas most uniformly interesting. I cannot imagine one's mentioning Kant or Hegel ; it is extremely improbable that anyone would mention even such masters of lucidity as Bentham or Sidgwick. For my own part I should think at once of some of the great English stylists—of Macaulay, of Froude, of Carlyle, of Hazlitt, of Lamb, of Ruskin (for special reasons I omit novelists and contemporaries). These men wrote in different ways and on different subjects—not always easy subjects by any means. But there is one

11

trait they all have in common : they are
unfailingly interesting. That makes one suspect that they have at least one other trait
in common, and with a little reflection one
finds it : what they wrote is saturated with
feeling. The emotions of these men, to be
sure, are most various ; but though their
feeling varies, there is no question of its
presence or its strength ; far from keeping
themselves out of what they write, they throw
themselves into it headlong ; they love and
hate publicly, eloquently, and with all their
hearts. Now we know that all the world
loves a lover, and Dr. Johnson knew that, like
himself, it loves a good hater. Readers want
their writers to make them feel alive, and
when they can sit with their authors and jeer
and laugh and scold and rejoice and admire
with them, they feel intensely alive.

Not one of the writers we have named could
be called exact or cautious in the handling of
ideas. Yet should any of us wish that these
writers had indeed kept themselves out of
their work ? Surely not. What makes their

style so attractive to us is precisely that with them style is so individually and revealingly the man. Carlyle without his mournfulness, his cackling derision, his pity for men generally and contempt for them in particular, and all the odd devices by which he smouldered and exploded into speech, would not only cease to be " the Rembrandt of English prose," he would cease to be Carlyle.

But consider how impossible all this is in philosophic writing. Philosophy is not an attempt to excite or entertain ; it is not an airing of one's prejudices—the philosopher is supposed to have no prejudices ; it is not an attempt to tell a story, or paint a picture, or to get anyone to do anything, or to make anyone like this and dislike that. It is, as James said, " a peculiarly stubborn effort to think clearly," to find out by thinking what is true. Any person who has made this attempt with the seriousness which alone justifies writing about it knows what an austere business it is. He knows that his hopes and fears and likes and dislikes are to

13

be rated philosophically at zero or worse, that they not only make no difference to the truth, but get in the way of his seeing it. Of course he has such feelings; he may well have become a philosopher precisely because he felt so strongly about these issues. But he realizes more clearly than most men that " things are what they are, and will be what they will be," whether he tears a passion to tatters about them or not. He knows from inner experience how often and how easily the needle of the compass is deflected away from truth by the presence in its neighbourhood of egotism, impatience, or the desire to score off somebody; and he would feel like a charlatan if he used on others methods he would resist in his own thinking. If he catches others in the attempt to use them on himself, his opinion of them plummets.

I must confess that often, when I have tried to read the most popularly effective of German philosophical writers, Nietzsche, I have felt like throwing the book across the room. He is a boiling pot of enthusiasms and animosities, which he pours out volubly, skilfully, and eloquently. If he were content to label these outpourings " Prejudices," as Mr. Mencken so truly and candidly labels his own, one could accept them in the spirit in which they were offered ; there is no more interesting reading than the aired prejudices of a brilliant writer. But he obviously takes them for something more and something better ; he takes them as philosophy instead of what they largely are, pseudo-Isaian prophesyings, incoherent and unreasoned Sibylline oracles.

Does it follow from all this that philosophers and their readers are doomed to roam a stylistic desert, and munch cactus as the sole article of their diet ? Happily the situation is not so desperate as that. It is true that the philosopher must live in a drier climate than most men would find habitable, and be content with what Bacon called the *lumen siccum* or dry light as distinct from the *lumen humidum*, or light drenched in the affections. But that is not necessarily fatal to the life of feeling ; even a rigorous austerity does not require that one's heart stop beating altogether. Of course if it did stop, one's thought would stop too. " Pure intellection," as Dr. Schiller used to say, " is not a fact in nature " ; our actual thinking is always moved by feeling and desire ; and unless these were felt by the writer, and somehow awakened and sustained in the reader, we should have nothing to-day to talk about. No philosopher is or can be a disembodied cerebrum ; what he is called on to exclude is not all emotions but only irrelevant emotions. That does exclude most applicants, including all the gaudier and more exciting ones, but it is not, after all, a clean sweep.

What is left him ? For one thing, the gusto he will feel in the business of thinking if he is really in love with his calling. Many philosophers have felt this, but found that it grows quickly cold when they put pen to paper. When it does come radiating through, it helps to keep the reader gratefully warm. Again, if a philosopher is a good human being, he knows that many of the beliefs he is attacking are intertwined inextricably with the hopes and feelings of those who hold them, and his controversial manner will take note of these involvements. Even if he thinks that religion and morals are the political progeny that flattery begets upon pride, he will know that this is hardly the most persuasive way of putting his case. The first examples that spring to my mind of this sympathy-rooted tact are not philosophers at all but theologians, in whom natural courtesy was perhaps vivified by Christian charity ; Dean Church and Cardinal Newman were fine exemplars of it, though Newman at times suddenly bared a tiger's claw. Among philosophers, one would surely nominate William James, " that ador-able philosopher," as Whitehead calls him, who could write a letter of vigorous expostula-tion in the most winning of terms. James suggests another respect in which philosophic writing may and should give evidence of feeling. The philosopher who discusses religion, as James did in the " Varieties," can hardly bring before his readers the thing he is talking about unless he has entered at first hand into an experience of deep feeling and can convey some idea of what this is like. James could do this because he had the needed resources of heart and speech. But how often writers on religion, morals, or art leave one with the bleak impression that they have never come within miles of what these experiences are like to the people who have them !

There is another kind of feeling, already touched on in passing, that I personally like in philosophic writing, though I admit the danger of it. It is not so much any single feeling as the range of feelings that answer to the degrees of elevation in the subject. Solemnity and the grand style in talking about the syllogism would deserve a laugh, and no doubt get it. But we have seen already that philosophy takes us at times into regions where feelings of a certain high kind are all but irrepressible. Kant, you will remember, confessed that he felt them when he thought of the moral law or the starry heavens; and when Pascal looked at those same heavens, he too broke out in the same way: " Le silence éternel de ces espaces infinis m'effraie."

If these little outbursts of great and rigorous thinkers stick in our minds, as they do, there is a reason for it. They are not excrescences or lapses; they live in our memories because, on the contrary, they are so natural, human, and just. Sir Thomas Browne said that he liked to pursue his reason to an *O Altitudo.* I follow him far enough to own that I like, in my philosophers, some responsiveness of mood to matter. With Mr. Garrod, I deplore the passing from among us of what he calls " magnificence of mind." It is the sort of presence you feel unmistakably in Plato, and I am not at all sure that it clouded those clear eyes. You feel it strongly in Spinoza, especially as his thought mounts towards its close and has to guard itself against breaking out with wings. Such feeling does not have to beg questions. The thinker who sees plainly, as Goethe did, that " existence divided

19

by human reason leaves a remainder," and a remainder of unimaginable dimensions, will not feel flip and jaunty as he faces it. In common-sense English writers this high semi-mystical seriousness is perhaps less natural than elsewhere, though it does break through at times. It is clearly present in Bradley's remark that for him metaphysics was a way of experiencing Deity, and that perhaps no one who did not feel this way had ever cared much for metaphysics. It is present again in that curious ground-swell of feeling that runs through the formal periods of T. H. Green, and still again in the organ notes of Mansel, that powerful but forgotten writer who was praised even by Pater for his " repression, with economy, of a fine rhetorical gift."

The mention of Dean Mansel reminds us that three of the greatest orators of modern times were teachers and writers of philosophy —Bossuet, Chalmers, and John Caird. They were all deeply religious men whose philosophy was an articulation of their faith, and as they were tremendous masters of the spoken word, they were irresistible when they could plead their case in person. Indeed if one wants an example of how far the oratorical manner can go, even when unsupported by matter, I should suggest that one look into Chalmers' *Astronomical Discourses*. He knew little enough about astronomy, but, convinced that the other planets were hovered over by angelic intelligences and were probably inhabited by souls more or less like ourselves, he prepared a discourse in whose very title we catch some echoes of his rolling periods : " On the Sympathy that is Felt for Man in the Distant Places of Creation." No doubt he swept his audience off their feet, and not improbably out of their senses. Here we have gone far over the line. Feeling and imagination, discontented with being servants and ministers to thought, have got quite out of hand and are leading it about by the nose.

The fact is that there is only one feeling that is always safe in thinking and writing about philosophy, and that is the one A. E. Housman has described as " the faintest of human

21

passions," the love of truth. This takes two forms, both of which are brought out in a sentence of Pater's, who was an attentive student of both philosophy and style. " In the highest as in the lowliest literature, then," he writes, " the one indispensable beauty is, after all, truth :—truth to bare fact in the latter, as to some personal sense of fact, diverted somewhat from men's ordinary sense of it, in the former ; truth there as accuracy, truth here as expression, that finest and most intimate form of truth, the *vraie vérité*." The love of truth in the first of these forms, the wanting to see the facts as they are, to follow the argument where it leads, even if it leads to the painful flouting of one's other wants, the readiness to consider all evidence, to give full weight to objections, to believe and admit that one has been wrong, this transparent honesty and objectivity of mind is rarer, I fear, even among philosophers, than pre-Freudians at least would have thought. It is a virtue more marked, perhaps, among empiricists than among rationalists. The philosophers who have displayed it in highest measure have not been the most consistent thinkers ; but even through palpable inconsistencies they have, by their disinterestedness and candour, kept a hold on their readers which the builders of more impressive systems might well envy. If a man is less concerned to see what is the case than to make out a case, if, whatever evidence is offered against him, his system absorbs it without a tremor, and goes on trumpeting its triumph, readers begin to suspect, even without definite evidence, that this is quite too good to be true.

It would be invidious to indict by name, where the evidence could only be equivocal, but it is not at all hard to name names on the other side. Of philosophers of high rank who have written in English, two of the most inconsistent are John Locke and John Stuart Mill. It is easy to criticize either of them, and many a wayside sharpshooter has put his little air gun in rest and scored palpable hits on them. But Locke and Mill, if I am not mistaken, are still with us, and still read with a will, while most of the sharpshooters are forgotten. This is not wholly because Locke and Mill stood on such a philosophic eminence. Surely it is partly because of the spirit in which they thought and wrote. Each had the enviable faculty of making people say : " If he is not right, at least he deserves to be ; he puts all his cards on the table ; he keeps nothing back ; he fights, thinks, and writes fairly, even to the point of writing clearly enough to be found out."

But it is with the love of truth in its other meaning that we are primarily concerned to-day, not so much the adjustment of thought to facts as the adjustment of expression to thought. The two are different and seem at times to fall apart. For example, John Dewey showed much of the former while deficient in the latter ; Cardinal Newman, I think, was rather deficient in the former while so exquisite a master in the latter that he gained credit for the former, too. However that may be, this love for the perfect accommodation of speech to thought is a rare thing, rarer, though less important, than the love of knowledge itself. It is the special feeling of the artist, the delight in creating a picture, a melody, a pattern of words, that will embody precisely and adequately, without loss or excess, what is in the maker's mind. An artist who lacked this interest would be a contradiction in terms; but there have been plenty of scientists and not a few philosophers who have lacked it almost wholly.

We must admit, therefore, that a philosopher can do without it; and since we are saying so much about style to-day, let me underline this remark by way of keeping our sense of proportion. " It is by style we are saved," said Henry James. That is simply not true in philosophy, at any rate at the top. There have been many powerful and athletic minds who would have regarded fastidiousness in style as effeminacy if not narcissism, and were far too engrossed with what they were saying to give much thought to how they were saying it. If there is anyone who reads Aristotle or Kant or Hegel or

Whitehead for the joy of perfect expression, I have still to hear of him. These men did not need style to save them, for they had something more important. I would go further and say that a preoccupation with style may sterilize a philosopher or even an artist. When an artist becomes so " abstract," so lost in pure form, that he has nothing left to express, he finds himself in a vacuum, and the step is not a long one from inanity to insanity. A philosopher who is precious, mannered, and self-conscious is a bore, either in person or on paper. But that style, though not all-important, is important nevertheless is plain enough if we pair some eminent names that naturally occur together. If you were to cover a stretch of a hundred pages in either Plato or Aristotle, which would you find more inviting ? If you knew that the same theory had been set out by Bradley and by Bosanquet, to which would you turn the more willingly ? The fact is that we want of our philosophers, as of our artists, both forms of the love of truth. " Subject without style," said

Professor Collingwood, " is barbarism ; style without subject is dilettantism. Art is the two together."

When we turn to look more closely at this craft of philosophic expression, we find to our relief that it is less exacting than the art of the true man of letters. What the philosopher must manage to embody in words is not the whole of him, nor the impulsive and imaginative part of him, but his intellectual part, his ideas and their connections. And his prime object must be to convey these to his readers at the cost of a minimum of effort on their part. He must get them to follow a process of distinguishing, abstracting, and inferring—in short, of thinking. That implies thinking on their part as well as his ; and thinking is hard work.

Now the way to save work for the reader is simply to write clearly. How easy it is to say that ! " Simply to write clearly "—as if that were not one of the hardest things in the world ! It is hard even to say what clearness means, let alone exemplify it in speech and writing. Indeed, there is no such thing if taken by itself; it lies in the relation between a giver-out and a taker-in. If there is trouble, it is sometimes wholly with the taker-in. Many a schoolboy has thought Euclid abominably obscure, and so he was—to the schoolboy. We have all known students who sat helpless before philosophers who were classics of clarity. On the other hand there are some purveyors of philosophy who pass all understanding, no matter whose. A master expositor, W. K. Clifford, said of an acquaintance: "He is writing a book on metaphysics, and is really cut out for it; the clearness with which he thinks he understands things and his total inability to express what little he knows will make his fortune as a philosopher." Unhappily, the gibe has point. There are philosophers, or pseudo-philosophers, to understand whom would be a reflection on the reader's own wit. But suppose, to revert to our opening illustrations, that the reader happens to be Macaulay reading Kant, or Reichenbach reading Hegel, or Russell reading the logician whom we quoted. If there is failure to understand in cases like this, it is not normally because the writer has nothing to say, and certainly not because the hearer is witless. The writer has simply failed to cross the bridge. Why ?

There are many reasons for such failure. One of the commonest is excessive generality in statement. Look at the statement by the eminent logician whom Russell had trouble with. One's thought has to travel so great a distance from the point where this generalization leaves it to the thing it is supposed to describe that it might lose itself in a hundred different directions before hitting on the right one. It is unjust, I grant, to tear a passage from its context in this way, and the context would undoubtedly help ; but if the context is of the same sort, that too will be obscure.

Listen to this from a great philosopher. I leave out only the first word and ask you to form the best conjecture you can of what he is talking about : " X is the self-restoration of matter in its formlessness, its liquidity ;

29

the triumph of its abstract homogeneity over specific definiteness ; its abstract, purely self-existing continuity as negation of negation is here set as activity." You might guess the writer of this—it is Hegel—but I would almost wager the national debt that you do not have the faintest suggestion of what he is actually talking about. Well, it happens to be heat—the good familiar heat that one feels in the sunshine or around fireplaces. I strongly suspect that this farrago is nonsense, but that is not my point. My point is that even if it is not nonsense, even if a reader, knowing that heat was being talked about, could make out, by dint of a dozen rereadings and much knitting of eyebrows, some application for the words, no one has a right to ask this sort of struggle of his reader.

Barrett Wendell, in his admirable book on writing, points out that clearness and vividness often turn on mere specificity. To say that Major André was hanged is clear and definite ; to say that he was killed is less definite, because you do not know in what way he was killed ; to say that he died is still more indefinite because you do not even know whether his death was due to violence or to natural causes. If we were to use this statement as a varying symbol by which to rank writers for clearness, we might, I think, get something like the following : Swift, Macaulay, and Shaw would say that André was hanged. Bradley would say that he was killed. Bosanquet would say that he died. Kant would say that his mortal existence achieved its termination. Hegel would say that a finite determination of infinity had been further determined by its own negation.

Some philosophers would surely do better here if they bore in mind what great writers seem to know by instinct, that a generalization which we can make without trouble if we are allowed to start from the bottom may be quite beyond us if we have to start from the top. Most of us are incapable of moving freely in the world of pure universals or " as suches " ; we are like Antaeus, and must touch ground again pretty often to renew our strength and courage. To be sure, there is some risk in such returns, for concrete things are complex, and if you are offered one as an example, you may pick out the wrong point in it. Kant was so convinced that this would happen that, for the most part, he deliberately abstained from illustrations. With all due respect, this seems to me rather silly. Most men's minds are so constituted that they have to think by means of examples; if you do not supply these, they will supply them for themselves, and if you leave it wholly to them, they will do it badly. On the other hand, if you start from familiar things, they are very quick to make the necessary generalizations. In a sense they are making such generalizations constantly; whenever they recognize the thing before them as a chair or a lamp-post, they are leaping from the particular to the general by a process of implicit classification.

How wrong Kant was is shown by the fact that even he finds it necessary at times to lapse into illustration, and that when he does, the going becomes strangely easier. Is the causal sequence temporal or not ? Put that question to the man who is at home in philosophy, and he will no doubt find it specific enough. Put it to the ordinary reader, and the chances are that you will draw a blank. Causality ? Temporality ? Nothing burgeons for him out of those dry sticks. Then try the tack that Kant, by a happy inspiration, did try. Instead of leaving the reader in mid-air to float down to the right case if he can find it, start him out with a particular case, a crucial one if possible, and let him see the general problem, and perhaps its solution, by himself. A lead ball is resting on a cushion. The pressure of the ball is causing a dent in the cushion. Is that situation clear ? Yes. Very well, does the dent come after the pressure that causes it or not ? That is the same problem as before. But what a difference in clearness and interest !

I said that in respect to clearness, empiricists come out on the whole better than rationalists. We can see now that this is no accident. Empiricists think that the meaning and test of thought lie in sensible experience, and hence they hover about this hearthstone much more closely than the far-ranging rationalists. Locke, Berkeley, and Hume are much more intelligible to most readers than their rationalist contemporaries, Spinoza, Leibniz, and Kant. Some philosophers of an empirical turn have speculated helpfully on what their advantage consists in. Charles Sanders Peirce, for example, wrote an essay on " How to Make Our Ideas Clear," which has had a very wide reading. Peirce links clarity and concreteness so intimately that he virtually reduces the one to the other ; he holds that unless there are particular things or events in experience at which one can ideally point and say " that is what I meant," one really means nothing at all. What does the theologian mean when he talks about God ? A being, he may say, that eye has not seen, nor ear heard, neither has it entered into the heart of man to conceive him. Exactly, Peirce would point out ; if you cannot see or hear or otherwise perceive him, you cannot conceive him either. What, if anything, then, does the word mean ? It means solely, Peirce would say, the differences that would be made in experience if God did exist; " Our idea of anything," he says, " *is* our idea of its sensible effects " ; " our conception of these effects is the whole of our conception of the object." Now this, as stated, does not, I think, make sense. If our thought of a thing is really exhausted in our thought of its sensible effects, to talk about the " it " that causes these effects must be meaningless. But what Peirce was trying to say has now been said rather more coherently by the positivists. Outside mathematics, they would say, to think and write clearly is to give every state-ment a reference to one distinct fact of sense perception ; a statement means the experience that would serve to verify it, and if there is no such experience, we are not really thinking about anything.

This doctrine seems to me at once deplorable philosophy and admirable literary advice. It is deplorable as philosophy because there are too many things that I can obviously think of which never have been or will be part of my own or anyone else's sense experience, such as your ideas as you listen to this, or the physicist's wavicles, or the relation of implication. But it is a useful admonition nevertheless, because if we cannot convert our generalizations on call into statements about particular instances, that does show in nine cases out of ten that we are not yet clear as to what precisely we are trying to say. If we are going to deal in paper money, let us at least be sure it is convertible into coin. The habitual practice of such conversion is one of the surest devices for responsible thinking and clear writing. On the logical side it serves to bring to light the instances that might shake or destroy our principle; and, as T. H. Huxley said, there is nothing like a sordid fact to slay a beautiful theory. On the expository side, it supplies a liberal chest of tools with which to sharpen and drive home our point. On this matter there are philosophers who might contemplate with profit the lively figure of Bernard Shaw. The " dismal science " of economics, with its complicated laws of price fixation and its still more complicated theory of international exchange, had long been a forbiddingly technical affair to the man who must do such reading in his slippers if at all. Shaw, in his *Intelligent Woman's Guide*, discussed these formidable problems in terms of a housewife shopping for frocks, and, to the pleased astonishment of thousands of readers, they became for the first time clear.

Among those readers there were no doubt students who asked, " Why don't philosophers write this way ? " In clarity, simplicity, movement, gusto, force, Shaw is indeed a model. But let us not be unfair to the philosophers. Put him beside such a writer as Sidgwick, and he divides at once into two persons, a rhetorical giant and a philosophical dwarf. Of course a man can write effectively if he is allowed to ride a high horse over qualifications and inconsistencies, and puff a case to twice its size by overstatement. But a philosopher cannot do that ; he must make his way cautiously along on foot, with a huge and crushing sack on his back labelled " Truth." It is notorious that some able and conscientious philosophers, because of these restrictions, have been virtually unable to move at all in their writing. But many aspiring writers of philosophy have failed for far less dignified reasons.

They have failed, for example, through carrying wrong models in the back of their minds. One influential teacher who writes badly can infect a whole brood of offspring, who proceed to spread the infection. Often our young philosophers, and still oftener our young psychologists and sociologists, are allowed to commit mayhem on the language unwarned, and to grow up under the innocent impression that such behaviour is somehow scholarly. " A spectre haunts our culture," says Lionel Trilling. " It is that people will eventually be unable to say, ' We fell in love and married,' let alone understand the language of *Romeo and Juliet*, but will, as a matter of course, say, ' Their libidinal impulses

38

being reciprocal, they integrated their individual erotic drives and brought them within the same frame of reference.' " Many of these young people carry no model in their minds by comparison with which they could stamp that sort of thing as barbarism.

But when philosophers fail in clarity, the cause may be quite different; it may be mere indolence, intellectual or literary. To carry thought and light through into the dark places of a subject is hard work; it is enormously easier to march through it to the sonorous sound of generalities. Descartes, you will remember, suggested that if we went wrong in our belief, it was really a moral matter; we allowed our wills to come to rest in a belief before our thought was clear about it. Without subscribing to so severe a doctrine, we can still agree that our bafflement as we read some writers on philosophy is not our fault at all, but due to the lack on their part of that last erg of energy needed to elicit an assumption or to make a distinction precise.

More easily remediable than intellectual

indolence, but still a fertile source of obscurity, is literary indolence, mere unwillingness to take the necessary pains. There have been many writers of philosophy in the past, there are many now, who, with great powers and much to say, say it so awkwardly, diffusely, and crabbedly, as to turn would-be readers away by their first page. They deserve to be heard and there are many who would like to hear them, but they hobble themselves by supposing that writing philosophy is merely philosophizing aloud. Now there are persons —I admire them from an immense distance— who have so trained themselves that they can cast their thought as they go into more than acceptable verbal form. Henry James dictated his later novels to Miss Bosanquet's clattering typewriter. And the incredible Hazlitt remarked about his own habit : " A practised writer ought never to hesitate for a sentence from the moment he sets pen to paper, or think about the course he is to take. . . . I ' unfold the book and volume of the brain,' and transcribe the characters I see there as mechanically as anyone might copy the letters in a sampler." But these are no ordinary mortals. It is safe to say that, on a subject of real difficulty, the form in which the thinking of most of us would first clothe itself would be shabby beyond all tolerance.

Writing philosophy involves two processes which with most men are bound to be separate —the process of manufacture and the process of packaging, the process of getting down on paper a first approximation to our thoughts, and the process of trimming, compressing, and furbishing, which makes it acceptable to consumers. There are few even of the master craftsmen who could afford to dispense with the latter process; and since we have named names on one side, we may do so on the other. We are assured on good authority that the impromptu letters of Sir Thomas Browne are astonishingly commonplace and those of Flaubert even shockingly faulty, showing how much their more formal writings owed to mere pains. The editor of the collection of Indian

41

Minutes on Education said that " scarcely five consecutive lines in any of Macaulay's minutes will be found unmarked by blots or corrections. . . . My copyist was always able instantly to single out his writing by the multiplicity of corrections and blots which mark the page." Newman confessed, " I have been obliged to take great pains with everything I have written, and often write chapters over and over again, besides innumerable corrections and interlined additions." It is written about the most spontaneous and readable of American philosophers, William James, that " whenever he was engaged upon any considerable piece of literary composition his letters to his friends grew full of groanings over the slowness and arduousness of his progress. He assures them that working all day and rewriting half a dozen times has only yielded him a page and a half of manuscript." " Everything comes out wrong with me at first," he said, " but when once objectified in a crude shape, I can torture and poke and scrape and pat it till it offends me no more."

You may say : " It is all very well to urge this energy with the blue pencil, but such advice has the very vagueness you have been deprecating. Energy is of no use unless one knows how to apply it, and just how and where is the blue pencil to be wielded ? " It is a fair demand, and I must try to meet it as best I can. Let us look first at the words used by philosophers, and then at their sentences.

We have seen how philosophic writing tends to excessive generality. It also tends at times, as Oxford philosophers have recently been pointing out, to play tricks with language, to use words in such a way as to suggest that the objects named by them fall in other categories than they do. Now abstractions are often hard to lay hold of, and there is something reassuring about good round noun substantives as names for them ; with such large placards on their backs they seem less elusive, less ethereal, easier to keep in sight. We have already heard Hegel saying in so many words that " reason is substance," and it seems as if in his world there is nothing

43

too impalpable to serve as a sort of substance. Perhaps at the outset A negates B, and X is finite, but before long negativity and finitude are off on their own, performing what Bradley described as " an unearthly ballet of bloodless categories." My first comment about words is that writers of philosophy might avoid some errors in thinking and lighten their manner if they were clearly aware of this tendency. I will call in aid here the invaluable H. W. Fowler : " Turgid flabby English of the kind common in inferior leading articles is full of abstract nouns ; the commonest ending of abstract nouns is *-tion* ; and to count the *-tion* words in what one has written, or, better, to cultivate an ear that without special orders challenges them as they come, is one of the simplest and most effective means of making oneself less unreadable."

I am not sure that philosophers are worse sinners in this respect than sociologists ; indeed I suspect the reverse. Here, at any rate, is an example of what a sociologist can achieve when warmed to his theme in an

article judged worthy of reprinting in a source-
book of sociology : " Social and political
organizations tend to become accommodated
to the spatial distribution or ecological
organization resulting from the prevailing
forms of transportation. The introduction of
new forms of communication such as the
railway, automobile, telegraph, radio, neces-
sitates a reaccommodation of social organization to the new interpretation of spatial
distance." Of the thirteen different nouns in
those two sentences, seven of them are -*tion*
nouns, and of these one, " organization,"
appears three times over. What is it that
makes civilized men do these things ? Often,
I am sure, a sense that what they have to say
is so commonplace that it must be dressed up
for dignity's sake, the sort of feeling that led
the American Collectors' Association, meeting
recently in Detroit, to announce that hence-
forth bill collectors preferred to be known as
" adjusters of delinquent obligations."

The enthusiasm for heavy substantives,
having spread from adjectives to -*ations*, is

now spreading backward again from -*ations* to adjectives. One distinguished philosopher talks to us about " the aspirational character of life." Another, in an able book, just off the press, writes, " a relation requires for its exemplification two or more particulars each of which must perform its special exemplificational function," and is on intimate terms with such strange new entities as " characteral features," and " punctuational commitments." In other writers I find it described how a philosopher approaches a problem " from the observational angle," how certain refugees coming to America had their " premigrational conceptions " changed, and how a certain kind of conduct is " organizationally cloaked with official piety." No doubt a case can be made out for such coinages on the ground that they take less space than the simpler words that might replace them. That may well be true. The case against them is that they are ugly misshapen verbal abortions.

The question has often been canvassed

whether it is better to write, in the main, in
Latin or in Anglo-Saxon. There is no doubt
that one's writing will have a different mood
or atmosphere as the one element of our
language or the other predominates. A critic
has suggested that if you want never to fail
in dignity, you should always use the generic
word rather than the specific; do not say,
" If any man strike thee on the right cheek,
turn to him the other " ; say, " If any injury
is done to thy person, do not indulge in
retaliation." There is a clear difference in
the tone of these two ; but you will note that
in converting from the specific to the general,
the writer has automatically translated into
Latin. Both components in the language are
important ; we could not do without either.
But just because philosophy runs to generality,
and has therefore a natural bent for the Latin,
the reader is the more surprised and pleased
when he finds it written in the homelier idiom.
Of course many writers have never thought of
asking whether their writing is predominantly
Roman or Saxon. It might pay them to

do so. Raleigh thought that "imperfect acquaintance with the Latin element in English is the cause of much diffuse writing and mixed metaphor. If you talk nonsense in Saxon you are found out at once; you have a competent judge in every hearer. But put it into Latin and the nonsense masquerades as profundity of abstract thought." Unfortunately the mask may deceive even oneself.

What about colour-words in philosophy, words that carry images with them or emotional overtones, the sort of words that poets use, or those writers who have written the gorgeous purple passages that get into our prose anthologies ? I must confess a weakness, if it is a weakness, for this sort of rhetoric ; indeed, when Burke or Sir Thomas Browne, De Quincey or Ruskin, lets out all the stops, one has to be pretty deaf not to hear. But one thing I feel sure about : this is not the way to write philosophy. It has often been tried, but never, I think, with much success. Plato, who is sometimes thought of as a philosopher of poetic mind, was on his guard against such writing; he distrusted poetry and imagery, and when he deserted plain prose, he preferred to do it with notice, and to go all the way over into myth.

The most distinguished recent exemplar of imaginative prose in philosophy is certainly George Santayana. Santayana was no man's copy, either in thought or in style. He consistently refused to adopt the prosaic medium in which most of his colleagues were writing. To read him is to be conducted in urbane and almost courtly fashion about the spacious house he occupies, moving noiselessly always on a richly figured carpet of prose. Is it a satisfying experience as one looks back at it ? Yes, undoubtedly, if one has been able to surrender oneself to it uncritically. But that, as it happens, is something that the philosophic reader is not very likely to do. Philosophy is, in the main, an attempt to establish something by argument, and the reader who reads for philosophy will be impatient to know just what thesis is being urged, and what precisely is the evidence for it. To such a reader Santayana seems to have a divided mind, and his doubleness of intent clogs the intellectual movement. He is, of course, genuinely intent on reaching a philosophic conclusion, but it is as if, on his journey there, he were so much interested also in the flowers that line the wayside that he is perpetually pausing to add one to his buttonhole. The style is not, as philosophic style should be, so transparent a medium that one looks straight through it at the object, forgetting that it is there ; it is too much like a window of stained glass which, because of its very richness, diverts attention to itself.

There is no reason why a person should not be a devotee of both truth and beauty ; but unless in his writing he is prepared to make one the completely unobtrusive servant of the other, they are sure to get in each other's way. Hence ornament for its own beautiful irrelevant sake must be placed under interdict. Someone has put the matter more compactly : " Style is the feather in the arrow, not the feather in the hat."

As for sentences, I shall say only one or two things that seem to me of especial importance in the writing of philosophy, and that I have not found much stressed in books on writing. The first has to do with the length of the sentence. If one is to have any rule about this, it must, I think, be a vague one, to the effect that each sentence should carry the thought one step forward. But what is to count as one step ? A sentence at its simplest makes one statement, but if we were to make only one statement per sentence, our writing would be unbearable. " Sir John came out of his house. He was in morning dress. He wore a top hat. He wore a monocle. He wore spats. He carried a cane. He hailed a taxi." Intolerable ! When details all hang together to make one picture, they can be grasped without difficulty as forming a single unit, and we throw them together into one sentence : " Sir John, radiant in morning dress, with top hat, monocle, spats, and cane, emerged from his door and hailed a taxi." But in regions of difficulty, it is a test of literary tact to know and take into account the length of the reader's stride. The ideal is a row of stepping-stones just far enough apart to enable him to keep moving without compelling him to make hops, skips, and jumps, still less leaps in the dark.

There are two common ways in which writers with more power than considerateness impose such efforts upon him. One is to leave out much-needed intermediate stones. A pupil of Laplace once said that when the lecturer introduced a statement with " now, gentlemen, it is evident that," he knew that a long later struggle would be required to see that it followed at all. I suspect that this was not so much a proof of intellectual brilliance on the teacher's part as of incompetent pedagogy. It is the business of the teacher or writer to insert the links that are needed if the hearer is to go along ; and I think we might well be less patient than we are with that lack of imagination which, through its very gaucheness, gets the reputation of brilliance and profundity. Persistently

52

obscure writers will usually be found to be defective human beings.

The second way of imposing an undue strain is to arrange the stepping-stones in groups so that one must skip about at awkward angles in one group before going on to the next. This is the method of the Teutonic sentence, the method of making each sentence into a miniature paragraph. Here is the sort of thing I mean, a sentence in which T. H. Green is making a not very difficult point : " Now it is because, to the real reformer, the thought of something which should be done is thus always at the same time the thought of something which he should be and seeks to be, but would not be if he did not do the work, that there is a real unity between the spiritual principle which animates him, and that which appears in the self-questioning of the man who, without charging himself with the neglect of any outward duty, without contemplating any particular good work which he might do but has not done, still asks himself whether he has been what he should be in doing what

he has done." There are few readers, I suspect, who are athletic enough to walk with
such seven-league boots. Bradley would have
broken the sentence up and made the matter
seem easy; he had an unusually sure sense
of how large an increment of thought he could
safely add in a sentence. By way of testing
my impression that Bradley ran to smaller
units than Green, I opened *Appearance and
Reality* and *Prolegomena to Ethics* at an
arbitrarily chosen page—I chose page 20—
and counted. On the page of Bradley I found
23 sentences averaging 16·4 words. On the
corresponding page of Green I found 12
sentences averaging 29·2 words; and not
only were Bradley's sentences much shorter;
the words in them were much shorter too.
I am sure that this difference in the unit-
mass of these two styles has something
to do with the heaviness of Green and
the comparative lightness and rapidity of
Bradley.

My second point about the sentence has to
do with its structure—not the grammatical

structure, which is discussed in the books on writing, but its rhythmical structure. My views here are perhaps old-fashioned. Many studies have been made of reading habits ; it has been found that one of the commonest causes of slow reading is the habit of saying the words as one reads, under one's breath ; and deliverance from such slowness is considered to lie in taking the meaning directly through the eye instead of receiving it at the end of a roundabout journey through the apparatus of speech. Remarkable results have been achieved by altering student habits in this respect ; in many cases the rate of reading has been doubled without loss in comprehension. Now for those who read solely through the eye, rhythm, which is addressed to the ear, must be of small concern. " Everybody writes prose for the eye nowadays," complained Logan Pearsall Smith, and added, " and it's quite dead."

But rhythm has been anything but a small concern to the masters of English prose. They plainly meant us to hear what they wrote. Perhaps in philosophy, where the difficulty of the thought usually compels slow going, the rule that Faguet set above all in his *L'Art de Lire, Lire lentement,* may still be accepted ; and where it is, rhythm becomes at once important for both writer and reader. Of course, both vary greatly in their sensitiveness to rhythm. There are philosophers and scientists of distinction whose writing is so uniformly cacophonous as to suggest either that they were congenitally lacking in the appropriate organ or that the suspicion of such a thing as rhythm had not occurred to them. One subvocal reader confessed that after reading the work of these performers for an hour or two, his jaw ached. On the other hand, there have been natural masters in prose who " lisped in numbers and the numbers came," who thought and wrote in measure, Thackeray and De Quincey, for example, and if more recent illustrations are wanted, the late H. W. Nevinson and Arthur Symons. To read such writers for sense only and not for sound is, I am persuaded, to miss not only

56

something very much worth having, but part of the sense as well.

For rhythm is one of the subtlest of all instruments in the delicate work of conveying thought. But there is one general rule that is at once so simple and so near the heart of the whole matter, that I must at least mention it.

This rule is to make the emphases of sense and rhythm coincide. Plain men know by a sort of instinct where to hit hard ; they never say, " There is in my mind a desire which would be gratified if you were to transfer the hammer into my possession " ; they say, " Give me the hammer." This is true style. Someone has said, " All peasants have style," and philosophers cannot afford to get wholly out of touch with the fine economy of natural talk. Consider this sentence from Mill : " To illustrate this farther, we may remember that virtue is not the only thing, originally a means, and which, if it were not a means to anything else, would be and remain indifferent, but which, by association with what it is a means to, comes to be desired for itself, and that too with the utmost intensity." No doubt one often stumbles along in this way in one's thinking, tacking on clause after clause not anticipated at the beginning, but there is little excuse for leaving the graph of one's meanderings on paper. Or take this, from so competent a writer as Dean Rashdall: "I may perhaps be allowed to remark that superficial observation of the facts would seem to suggest that, while certain moral capacities or incapacities can scarcely be separated from those physical and intellectual characteristics which are undoubtedly inherited, it is questionable whether the fully-developed moral belief or 'intuition' could be transmitted to offspring apart from the influence of education and environment."

One need only consider such sentences as these to feel the truth of John Morley's remark, "It is a great test of style to watch how an author disposes of the qualifications, limitations, and exceptions that clog the wings of his main proposition." In both the sentences just quoted, the authors have boggled over this, with the result that incidentals are unduly stressed, and the march of the argument slowed down. The beginning of a sentence is a position second only to the end in importance; but note how Rashdall wastes it with the cumbrous " I may perhaps be allowed to remark that superficial observation of the facts would seem to suggest . . ." Now look at a sentence that shows us how to waste the end ; it is from an eminent living expert on the philosophy of language : " It is not surprising that Hume, who had declared war on the same conceptions, should make a suggestion that may be regarded as one historical fountainhead of the relational theory of mind, nor that he himself should abandon it because of an inconsistent retention of the very categories which he ostensibly opposed— a retention whose influence has already been discussed in connection with his skeptical and subjectivistic tendency." What down-at-heel stuff that is, shambling and shuffling along as if it had no notion where it was going, or whether, perhaps, it might not have got there already. The point we are making has been made by Hazlitt, and since Hazlitt was a man with an ear, we may profit by knowing how he put it : " No style is worth a farthing that is not calculated to be read out, or that is not allied to spirited conversation." Not Hazlitt at his best, but pith and force itself as compared with the mumbling we have just heard. Note how the runs of syllables, " calculated to be *read out*," " that is not allied to *spirited conversation*," end in a repeated and pounding emphasis on the words that carry the main meaning. That is the way live men naturally talk. If their writing too is to be alive, it is the way they must write.

Regarding units larger than the sentence, there is less need to speak. Some philosophers write to plan and scale ; their heads and sub-heads are worked out in advance, and they follow them as a lawyer does his brief. I find other philosophers reporting that such planning is impossible for them, that they discover what they think only as they write, and that

the arrangement of the whole must be deferred
to the end, when they examine the amorphous
thing to which they have given birth and tidy
it up as best they can.

It is surprising that one obvious method
of arranging one's matter has been used
so seldom, and then so rarely with success.
Philosophy, as Plato said, is a kind of dialogue
of the soul with itself, and the dialogue,
expertly used, is an effective way of winding
one's course through a subject. But it is a
far more difficult and treacherous method than
it seems. Try to make it dramatic by accen-
tuating the characters and their idiom, and
the philosophic reader feels that he is being
dragged off into irrelevancy for the sake of a
frivolous brightness; make your characters
into mere philosophic abstractions, and, like
all other abstractions, they will be dead. I
can think of only three writers who have
handled the dialogue form in philosophy with
conspicuous success—Plato himself, Berkeley,
and Lowes Dickinson; and the exactingness
of the form is suggested by the fact that these

men were all masters of expression outside this particular form.

Berkeley proved against all the Heideggers of the world that philosophy can be written clearly, against all the Hegels that it can be written simply, against all the Kants that it can be written with grace. He was no mere popularizer ; he was an acute, original, and technical thinker, urging a theory that is about as shocking to common sense as any theory ever offered. But though even Dr. Johnson could not answer him, the plain man could read him and understand. " I shall throughout endeavour," he wrote, " to express myself in the clearest, plainest, and most familiar manner, abstaining from all hard and unusual terms which are pretended by those that use them to cover a sense abstracted and sublime." He kept to this engagement. He " spoke with the vulgar " without ceasing to think with the learned. Like G. E. Moore in our own day, he showed in the one wholly convincing way—by example—that philosophy could maintain all the sharp-eyed wariness

of the specialist while walking the road of
ordinary speech.

In spite of Berkeley and all his works, there
will be some who continue to think that this
matter of style is unworthy of a philosopher's
pains. They even have some good writers on
their side. " People think that I can teach
them style," said Matthew Arnold. " What
stuff it all is ! Have something to say and
say it as clearly as you can. That is the only
secret of style." And Samuel Butler, an
excellent writer himself and the teacher of
Shaw, said : " I never knew a writer yet who
took the smallest pains with his style and was
at the same time readable. . . . Men like
Newman and Stevenson seem to have taken
pains to acquire what they called a style as
a preliminary measure—as something that
they had to form before their writings could
be of any value. I should like to put it on
record that I never took the smallest pains
with my style, have never thought about it,
and do not know or want to know whether it
is a style."

I respect the judgment of these men, but cannot agree with it. The best way to decide the matter is to read those writers—in our case those philosophers—who did take pains with their style and compare them with those who did not.

Philosophy is no respecter of persons. An argument is not the more valid because offered by one man rather than another, or eloquently rather than awkwardly; we need hardly say that it is not only idle, it is wrong, to try to make such an argument valid by verbal dressing. But philosophy, while an impersonal subject, is thought and written by persons. The brains of these persons, when they think, are not dynamos humming in a vacuum; actual thought is always bathed in personal feeling, and invested with the lights and shades of an individual temperament. Now much of the pleasure of reading lies in catching the special quality of one's author, and so making his acquaintance. Think how the differing temperaments of Addison and Swift, of Mencken and Chesterton

come to us through their words. They do not
pretend to give us merely the facts. They
convey in a thousand ways how the facts
strike them. And most people are so constituted that facts are far more vivid and
interesting if they come wearing the stamp of
another's interest across their face. There is
nothing sinister in this ; they need not be the
less interested in the argument because they
are also interested in the author. Should any
of us wish that Hobbes were less unmistakably
Hobbes in his writing, or Bradley Bradley, or
Moore his repetitious, lucid, vehement, pains-
takingly precise self ? No doubt we could
still get the drift of their argument if these
men all wrote alike. But we do not want
them to write alike. We want to hear the
man in and through the thought, and as
Buffon said, " The style *is* the man."

Or at least it may be. Here Arnold and
Butler, I suggest, were wrong. A style that
expresses one's mind adequately is not
achieved by nature or accident, but only by
pains. Was it not Charles Lamb who said

that when we look in a mirror we dislike what we see, but hope to make up for it by something in our expression ? Well, fully to make up for our wooden outsides, to express flexibly what is within, is a prodigious business. The style of a true writer, says Newman, is " the faithful expression of his intense personality, attending on his own inward world of thought as its very shadow : so that we might as well say that one man's shadow is another's as that the style of a really gifted mind can belong to any but himself. It follows him about *as* a shadow. His thought and feeling are personal, and so his language is personal."

Now thought and feeling are so bound up with expression that it is only by observing their expression year after year and experimenting with it freely that we discover what we are really like. If you were to ask any of the master-craftsmen who are known for styles that are deeply and personally expressive, like that of Newman himself, you would find, I think, that every one of them had a history of long apprenticeship and experimentation. One thinks of Stevenson, " the sedulous ape," of the strange gap between the early Carlyle and the writer who burst on the world in *Sartor Resartus*, of Philip Guedalla's untrue but unforgettable history of Henry James as "James the First, James the Second, and James the Old Pretender." These men kept on experimenting till at last they found their own medium.

One last point : Whitehead went so far as to say, "Style is the ultimate morality of mind." That is a startling statement. But if we think of style in the large way in which Pater was thinking of it when he said it had a double aim of complete fidelity to fact and to one's complex sense of fact, we can perhaps see what Whitehead meant. We are shooting at a star when we aim at style in this sense ; we are trying to do justice at once to an infinity without and a near infinity within. Even the writers that have gone furthest towards the goal in some respects fall notably behind in others. The most unfailingly lucid writer in the history of English literature is

Macaulay, whose speeches in particular are masterpieces of incisive statement. The trouble is, as Augustine Birrell once remarked, that you cannot tell the truth in Macaulay's style. In satisfying his passion for clarity, he allows himself to omit shades and qualifications that are there in the facts, but would smudge his sharply etched lines if he were to put them into his picture. His style is the embodiment of his mind, and his mind, with all its learning, its delight in learning, and its extraordinary gift of communicating both, is a mind that moves on the surface of things and shies away instinctively whenever it perceives a depth or feels a mystery ; it "marches through the intricacies of things in a blaze of certainty." The defects in Macaulay's mind forced themselves into his manner, and showed that the only way to amend that remarkable style was to be a better mind and a better man.

So in the end of all of us. The more perfectly one's style fits the inner man and reveals its strength and defect, the clearer it becomes that the problem of style is not a problem of words and sentences merely, but of being the right kind of mind. " He who would not be frustrate in his hope to write well in laudable things," said Milton, " ought himself to be a true poem." Does that make the problem of style insoluble ? Yes, I am afraid it does. But it shows also that the problem we have been discussing is no petty or merely technical one, but very far-reaching indeed. We may have to agree with Professor Raleigh that " to write perfect prose is neither more nor less difficult than to lead a perfect life."

BEEKMAN
COLLEGE
LIBRARY

DISCARD